This book is dedicated to Adia-Tuesday,
the most curious kid I know.

Tuesday Books, Melbourne.

Copyright © Clio Gates Foale 2020.

All rights reserved. No part of this book may be reproduced, transmitted or stored in an information retrieval system in any form or by any means, graphic, electronic or mechanical, including photocopying, taping and recording, without written permission from the copyright owner.

WHOSE POO ARE YOU?

A guide for tiny zoologists.

Written and illustrated by Clio Gates Foale.

This book is all about **poo!**

Can you guess who these poos belong to?

This poo is **large**, wet and brown or dark green.

Whose **poo** are you?

Emu's poo!

Emus swallow **stones** and keep them in their stomach to help grind up their food!

This poo is small and round. If you give it a sniff it smells like **gum leaves**.

Whose **poo** are you?

This poo is long and narrow, about the size and shape of a **thumb**.

Whose **poo** are you?

This poo is full of ants, termites and **sand**. The ends are crumbly and broken.

Whose **poo** are you?

This poo is sloppy, **stinky** and full of seeds.

Whose **poo** are you?

This poo has brown **mushy** bits and white smeary bits.

Whose **poo** are you?

This poo is black on the outside but it is green, dry and **grassy** on the inside.

"I'm about the size of a prune."

Whose **poo** are you?

This poo is black and very small, about the size of a **raisin**.

Whose **poo** are you?

This poo is black or dark green and is shaped like a **cube**.

Whose **poo** are you?

With all this pooping going on, why aren't we stepping in steaming piles of poo everywhere we go?

You can thank **DUNG BEETLES!**

Some dung beetles eat the poo, other dung beetles bury the poo.

About the author and illustrator

Clio Gates Foale studied Zoology at the University of New South Wales, Sydney and has worked as an ecologist in Melbourne for 15 years. She has been pooped on by many of Australia's native animals, and a few internationals just for luck.

Acknowledgements

Thanks to **Kim Downs** (mammal expert), **Barry Goldsmith** (snake expert), **Alexia Gates-Foale** (animation expert), **Rachel Brown** (design expert), **Jessica Window** (wife) and **Ballarat Wildlife Park** for making sure this book is full of it.

My biggest thanks go to **Christine Gates** for letting me cut up and collage her artwork to create the patterns and backgrounds you see on these pages. Look up **Christine Gates Fine Art** to see her original work!

Photo credits

Kangaroo: David Foale, Hunter Valley, NSW.
Tiger Snake: Barry Goldsmith (Victoria Snake Catcher). RIP George the Chappell Island Tiger Snake. He lived 13 great years. This is a photo of his last ever poo.
Wombat: Chris Kaskadanis, Mt Disappointment, Victoria.
All other photos by Clio Gates Foale.

www.ingramcontent.com/pod-product-compliance
Lightning Source LLC
Chambersburg PA
CBHW061136010526
44107CB00068B/2958